To Fred

The Sierra Club, founded in 1892 by John Muir, has devoted itself to the study and protection of the earth's scenic and ecological resources — mountains, wetlands, woodlands, wild shores and rivers, deserts and plains. The publishing program of the Sierra Club offers books to the public as a nonprofit educational service in the hope that they may enlarge the public's understanding of the Club's basic concerns. The point of view expressed in each book, however, does not necessarily represent that of the Club. The Sierra Club has some sixty chapters in the United States and in Canada. For information about how you may participate in its programs to preserve wilderness and the quality of life, please address inquiries to Sierra Club, 85 Second Street, San Francisco, CA 94105.

First U.S. Edition 1996

First published in Canada by Greey de Pencier Books Inc., 179 John Street, Suite 500, Toronto, Ontario M5T 3G5

Library of Congress Cataloging-in-Publication data is available from Sierra Club Books for Children, 85 Second Street, San Francisco, CA 94105.

Book design and art direction by Julia Naimska

Printed in Hong Kong

10 9 8 7 6 5 4 3 2 1

Wild
in the
City

Jan Thornhill

Sierra Club Books for Children
San Francisco

AS THE SUN GOES DOWN, night creeps quietly into the city. Streetlights blink on, making big yellow circles on sidewalks and lawns.

Jenny's mother is tucking her in when Jenny hears a strange sound coming through the open window.

"What's that?" she asks her mother.

"I don't hear anything," her mother answers.

"Listen!" whispers Jenny. "It sounds like *churr, churr, churr.* Can't you hear it?"

They both hold their breath and listen very hard. They hear leaves rustling in the breeze, the faraway honk of a horn, a dog barking. And then, nothing.

"Maybe you imagined it," says Jenny's mother.

"No, there was something out there," Jenny insists. "Maybe a wild animal!"

"Well, it's not there now," says her mother, as she kisses Jenny goodnight. "And it's time for you to go to sleep."

In the tree just outside Jenny's window, a mother raccoon and her three fluffy kits climb down to the ground.

Churr, churr, churr, chatter the kits as they scramble after their mother, over fences and across backyards. They follow her up onto a porch where she stops in front of a bowl of dry cat food. The kits watch closely as their mother dips a piece of food in the cat's water bowl and gently turns it. All at once, the raccoon family is startled by a loud, deep *whirr* overhead. They look up into the starry night sky.

High above them, a sleek nighthawk soars through the air, searching for mosquitoes and other flying insects to eat. Suddenly he spots a fat, fuzzy moth. Folding his wings against his sides, he dives straight down. Then, *whirr,* he spreads his wings and swoops sharply upward. *Peent! Peent! Peent!* he cries as he closes in on his prey. But the nighthawk is not the only one hunting on the wing. A small, dark shadow darts out and snatches the moth away.

It's a little brown bat. She swallows the moth and keeps right on flying. All through the darkest, quietest hours of the night, she flits about, catching as many insects as she can.

Circling a house once, twice, three times, the bat senses movement far below. Curious, she dives down to investigate. But the little moving things aren't tasty flies or swarming gnats. They are bits of torn grass being tossed into the air.

A skunk is looking for June bug grubs to eat. The grass flies up as he digs with his long claws to get at the juicy larvae in the soil. He digs and eats his way across the lawn until he reaches the alleyway, where he finds a big, green bag full of garbage. He rips a hole in the bag, rummages through it, and pulls out a chicken bone.

As the sky turns from inky black to deep blue, the sleepy skunk waddles toward his den under the porch. He turns a corner and stops short. Another animal stands in his way!

A cat stares curiously at the skunk, then gingerly moves one step closer. The skunk stamps his front feet in warning and raises his tail in the air. The cat slinks away to explore other backyards and alleys. Keeping her eyes sharp and her ears cocked, she roams the neighborhood, as wild and free as a tiger in the jungle.

As the sky brightens near dawn, the cat's stomach begins to growl. By now there should be fresh food in her bowl. Returning home, she pads up the steps to her back door and meows loudly. Up above her, there is rustling in a tree. Her ears twitch and turn at the sound, but just then the door opens. As the cat purrs her way into the house, a waking bird begins to sing.

Cheer-up, cheerily! A robin
greets the sun as it peeks between
the houses. Close by, his mate ruffles her
feathers as she awakens on their nest.
Four hungry chicks stir beneath her.

The mother robin flies off in search
of insects for her nestlings. She returns
with a grasshopper, and all four chicks
cheep loudly, beaks gaping wide. She
feeds two of the chicks and sets out
again. A flash of wings catches her eye.
She gives chase, but suddenly her prey
seems to vanish into thin air.

The mourning cloak butterfly has landed on a tree trunk. She is almost impossible to spot, because her closed wings are the same color as the brown bark of the tree. After a while, she flutters into the park across the street.

The butterfly flits from tree to tree, looking for just the right place. Finally she alights on a sun-warmed branch and begins to lay her pale eggs. She has just laid her fourteenth egg when the branch starts to tremble. Startled, she opens her wings and flies away.

A gray squirrel scampers along the branch. As she reaches the end, she makes a flying leap into another tree. Scurrying among its leaves, she nibbles on bugs and beetles, then disappears into a hole in the tree trunk.

Inside, her five babies chatter excitedly. The mother squirrel curls up with them in their cozy nest of leaves and shredded newspapers. One by one, the babies nuzzle up to her, looking for milk. The squirrel family is too busy to notice a bright pair of eyes peering in at them.

But the house sparrow moves on. She flies here and there, looking for another place to make her home. After a long search, she discovers a perfect spot under the eaves of a house.

As the afternoon sun burns brightly, the sparrow finds grasses and twigs to build her nest. Suddenly, a dark shadow comes between her and the sun. A hunting bird is swooping down toward her! Frightened, she darts left, then right to escape the bigger bird.

Still hungry, the kestrel lands on top of a tall building. From his high perch, he can see all around. As the sun sinks low in the sky, he spots a female kestrel on another rooftop.

Killy-killy-killy! he cries as he glides toward her. He flies around and around in circles, inviting her to be his mate. As he finally settles beside her on the rooftop, one of his feathers flutters down to a garden far below.

The feather lands on the back of a sleeping toad, waking him up. He takes a slow hop forward, then stops. Some ants are crossing the garden path. In a flash, he flicks out his long, sticky tongue. When he snaps it back, a tiny ant is stuck to the tip of it.

As the toad eats ant after ant, the sun sinks slowly behind the houses and trees. When the streetlights blink on, the toad feels the ground start to shake. Something big is coming!

Jenny and her mother walk up the path to their house. It's Jenny's bedtime.

Upstairs, they both hear the same strange sound Jenny heard the night before.

"Listen!" says Jenny. "There it is again!"

This time they go to the window and look out. There, in the tree outside Jenny's window, is the mother raccoon with her three fluffy kits. Jenny and her mother watch the raccoon family climb down the tree and frolic in the backyard. Then, when the last striped tail has disappeared into the darkness, they hold their breath and listen hard.

For a few moments, they can still hear the soft *churr, churr, churr* of the raccoons. But finally that, too, fades into the night.

NATURE NOTES

If you live in a city or town, you may not be aware of the wild creatures that live around you. But there are sure to be some! If you look and listen carefully, you may see them or find signs that they are there. When you set out to explore your neighborhood for signs of wildlife, remember that you should *never* approach an animal you don't know. Even though it may look tame, stay away from it, for its safety as well as your own.

RACCOONS

In cities, raccoons raise their young in chimneys, attics, and garages, as well as in hollow trees. At night, they roam through neighborhoods looking for food. In the wild, raccoons forage in and around streams for crayfish and turtle eggs. In the city, however, they rummage through garbage and feast on food left out for pets. Raccoons like to feel their food with their hands before they eat it. They will also "wash" their food if they can find water. The reason for this behavior is not known.

You might hear raccoons at night, making chattering, churring, or growling sounds.

NIGHTHAWKS

Nighthawks came to live in cities when people began using gravel on rooftops more than one hundred years ago. The gravel is a lot like the pebbly ground they like to nest on in the wild. During courtship and nesting, the male nighthawk will dive down very close to his mate, then swoop up again. The air rushing between his longest wing feathers makes a deep whirring noise.

Not really hawks at all, nighthawks were named for the hawklike way they hunt insects on the wing. One nighthawk can catch as many as five hundred insects in one night.

LITTLE BROWN BATS

The bat is the only mammal that can truly fly. Each wing is a thin sheet of muscle and skin stretched between the bat's body, arm, and long fingers. As the little brown bat flies, it makes high-pitched squeaks. The sound waves bounce off insects and echo back into the bat's ears. The bat's brain uses the echoes to make a "sound picture" that helps it hunt in the dark.

Little brown bats sleep during the day. In the country, they hide in crevices behind tree bark or in cracks in large rocks. City bats sleep between loose shingles and under eaves.

SKUNKS

In both city and country, skunks leave their dens when night falls. They eat insects and their larvae, fruits, small mammals, and eggs. Skunks that live near people's homes often pick through garbage for food. A skunk shows little fear of other animals. This is because it can spray its enemies with a foul-smelling liquid from two glands near its tail.

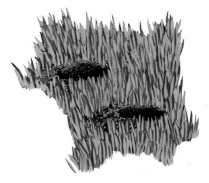

Besides the animal's strong smell — and tracks found in the mud or snow — the best signs that a skunk lives nearby are shallow holes in the earth. Skunks dig them looking for insects. Often several holes will be found close together.

ROBINS

Robins are woodland birds, but they came to live near people when good nesting trees were planted in cities and towns. Robins eat mostly insects, but they also like earthworms. Worms are easier for robins to find on dewy lawns than on the forest floor.

If you find a baby robin that has fallen from its nest, be sure to leave it alone. Its parents are probably nearby, and they will feed it until it learns to fly and fend for itself.

MOURNING CLOAK BUTTERFLIES

Mourning cloaks are often the first butterfly of spring. They hibernate under tree bark through the winter, until the weather warms. The female lays eggs on poplars, elms, and other trees planted in cities. A caterpillar hatches from each egg and eats leaves until it is big enough to form a chrysalis. Inside the chrysalis, the caterpillar changes into a butterfly and emerges after a few weeks.

GRAY SQUIRRELS

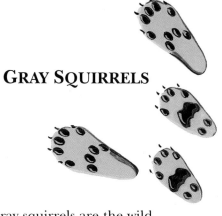

Gray squirrels are the wild animals you are most likely to see during the day. Even in cities and towns, they feel safe high in the treetops. In spring, they eat buds and tree flowers; in summer, fruit and insects; and in fall and winter, nuts and seeds. Squirrels don't remember where they bury their nuts, but they can smell them through even a thick layer of snow.

In bare winter trees, it's easy to spot the "dreys" where squirrels sleep in the summer. Squirrels build these basketball-size nests out of sticks and leaves. They line them with grasses, feathers, and, in cities, paper and other soft trash.

HOUSE SPARROWS

House sparrows were brought to North America from England in the 1850s to control insects. Their numbers grew quickly, and before long they were thriving from coast to coast.

House sparrows are cavity nesters, and they have no trouble finding nesting sites in urban nooks and crannies. They stuff whatever crevice they can find with grasses, weeds, and trash. They line their nests with feathers, hair, and string. To find a sparrow's nest, look for grass hanging from behind shutters and signs and from the eaves of houses.

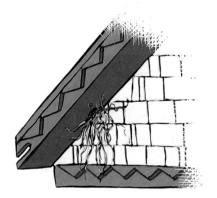

KESTRELS

The kestrel, North America's smallest falcon, hunts insects, rodents, and small birds. As more and more house sparrows made their homes in cities, so did kestrels. A kestrel will often hover in the air, high above a scurrying mouse or a pecking bird, then plunge down suddenly to take its victim on the ground.

In the wild, kestrels nest in hollow trees, but in cities they look for nooks and crannies in the eaves of buildings.

TOADS

Toads are normally found on dry land, but they must return to water to lay their eggs. Toad eggs look like frog eggs, but they are laid in long, slimy ribbons. Many North American toads can blend in with their surroundings by changing the color of their skin — they can go from light to dark, or from mottled to a more solid color. At night, toads are drawn to lights, where they feed on the insects that are attracted to the brightness.

CATS

Many house cats live in two worlds — indoors and out. Indoors, we feed and play with them. But outdoors, even the gentlest cat can behave more like a wild animal, killing and eating small mammals, birds, and insects. When you play with a cat by rustling paper or rolling a ball along the floor, you bring out its hunting instincts. The cat acts as if the toy is alive, and, like its wild relatives, it will stalk and pounce.

NAME GAME

Jenny's cat is the only animal in this book that has been given a name. Look closely and you will see Jenny's black-and-white cat in every illustration. Look even more closely to find one letter hidden in each illustration. Find all thirteen hidden letters and you will spell the cat's name.